from The

Angels of Light

Poems, Prayers and Powerful Words

by

Melissa O'Neill

Independently Published on Amazon by CKB Press

13 Shannon Cove, Dromod,
Co. Leitrim, Republic of Ireland
Email: info@ckbpress.com
Website: www.ckbpress.com

First Edition

ISBN-: 9798653464133

Book credits

Photos by various photographers on unsplash.com.

Dedication

This book is dedicated to my Mother Alice Murray and my deceased grandmother Mary O'Brien.

These two amazing women introduced prayer into my life at a very young age, and for that, I thank them.

I know the power of prayer and how it helped me in my life.

A big tribute to these ladies who have spread the love and light.

What people are saying about Rainbow Messages from the Angels of Light.

This book is light, gentle and an uplifting read, well versed and taught out which brings a pure essence to it.

Garreth

The words are so amazing and enlightening, and the artwork is so beautiful. The prayers are so beautifully written and so easy to understand. The words in the book are so powerful, and when you say them out loud, you can feel them coming from your heart as if your heart was in a flutter. You can feel the radiance of the Angel's come to you and sharing their love to you. I will be using it in my everyday life, and I highly recommend it to everyone to buy it and read it as it will help you get through some difficult times. The Angels are always there for us and always brings our message to God xx

Maria Whelan

Melissa is a wonderfully gifted and spiritual human being. This collection of insightful thoughts, prayers and poetry acts as magical beacon of hope and encouragement during troubled times. There is real wisdom in each of the beautifully crafted poems and prayers. Melissa's words are uplifting, encouraging and provide insightful spiritual guidance. The book is a precious gift which will support the reader in negotiating this sometimes challenging and often magical journey through a lifetime.

Eoin

Such beautiful content of poems and quotes. It wrapped me in warmth while reading, feeling my angels whom I call on ever closer to me. Shine Bright 😊 🖤

Deirdre Thornton

I really enjoyed all aspects of this book. The use of images throughout were perfect and fit really well with how the book reads. The quotes used throughout the book are inspiring and uplifting, and many have helped me with my outlook on my current situation. I found that I learned more about the angels from this book than I expected to, and this was very interesting. I loved the poems and prayers within the book and found them really insightful. This book brought me a lot of inner peace as I read it, and I will continue to look back on this when I feel I need to. I would recommend this book to anyone with an interest in this or anyone who is looking for a book that will help them with any internal struggles they may have. Well done Melissa it is amazing.

Cliona

I really enjoyed the book. You should be so proud. I cannot imagine the work that went into it. I had no idea there were so many angels, and the different light is new to me also. Also, the pictures were perfect. I felt they had a very calming influence and resonated with me as I was reading.

Great job! What a fantastic achievement. You have a gift.

Brenda

I have finished reading your wonderful book. I honestly did not realise there were so many angels for so many areas and struggles in life. I thoroughly enjoyed reading it, and you should be so proud of your work. I also loved the quotes, which I feel everyone can relate to on different levels. For me, Gabriel seemed a comfort and also Uriel. Your images consistently portray peace and calm. I think you've done a tremendous job and I would have no hesitation in recommending this book to any friend who needed some guidance.

Aine McCarthy Vigors

I love it. I very much love affirmations, prayers and manifesting and this is beautiful! Thank you for sharing with me - I hope it does really well!

Jess

Reading these powerful quotes, poems and prayers is a positive and inspiring way to start every day. Each poem and prayer carries an uplifting message. It is beautifully presented with lovely images used throughout. This book is recommended for those looking for peace through prayer and poetry.

Brian

Rainbow Messages from the Angels of Light is a beautifully written piece of work.

It is a stunning book of prayers, poems, messages and quotes that have come through to Melissa from her Angels and Guides,

This book is written in simplistic terms and is suitable for both adult, young adult and children alike. The messages are very powerful and spiritual.

It is a very comprehensive little book that has a very gentle way of connecting one to the Healing Energy of the Angels, God, Our Divine Higher Power, or whatever way, you the reader, connects to Source.

The poems, messages, prayers and quotes are uplifting, easily understood and to the point.

The wording of this terrific book are spiritual, powerful, healing and magical, while being subtle and gentle at the same time.

Rainbow Messages from the Angels of Light

is an absolute wonderful read to which I've been very honoured and privileged to be asked to review for and on behalf of my beautiful friend Melissa.

Mary Ivers

About the Author

My name is Melissa O Neill. I am a holistic therapist living in the beautiful garden county of Ireland.

I work closely with the Angelic Realm and the fifteen Archangels and my Guardian Angels who guide me.

This close connection with the angels is how this book has been produced. I give thanks to the angels of the light, gods angels and the guidance they have given me to write this book.

I am currently writing my second book on the angels (volume 2) with the help of the angels. I will channel and create some downloadable meditations to go with this book. You will be able to find them on my website which will be available at the end of the year.

To avail of any of my services you can connect with me personally through my website

www.melissashealing.ie

or on Facebook at Melissa's healing.

Love and Blessings to you all.

Melissa

"Staying positive in love and light, ignites the happiness for us all in life."

About this book

Angels are beings of light.

They will not interfere with you unless called upon. You were born with free will, and they know you have free will and choice.

It is your divine right to be happy.

The angels want to help and serve you in all ways.

Angels will help you open to the light love, truth and compassion that is within you. They vibrate on many rays of light and shades of colour. They have their own abilities to help in certain areas, but all will bring you to the divine light to open the hearts to love and light.

They will help you see the divine light in you, so you can open fully to the love within you to love yourself first. Then you can emanate that love around to all other people. This way, you can see and make choices that serve you for your soul and life's purpose.

The angels are light, gentle, but powerful

energies that can lead you to a life of peace and harmony.

Angels will help you on many roads that you take.

They are compassionate and love you, unconditionally.

There is no judgement they will serve whenever you ask for help or call upon them for assistance.

You can connect with the angels through prayer and words, an intention to connect.

Prayer is powerful

Prayer is sacred.

Prayer is an intention.

Prayer is a way to open for support to the divine god, the divine beings of light.

Prayer is peaceful.

Prayer lets us focus on what we need to help us right now.

Prayer is a form of meditation that brings peace and comfort.

4

Prayer is healing.

All the challenges and experiences in life are stepping-stones to raise us higher as we learn and grow.

We build blocks as we go.

We may experience suffering this will help us grow.

We may experience pain, hurts, sorrow, and challenges as we go.

All your prayers will be heard and answered. Angels are listening and are there to support, guide, protect and love us unconditionally.

The power of intention is powerful. When we call on the angels for support, our prayers are heard and answered.

Look, listen and learn

Poem

Many shades of darkness

murky and grey

wallowing in the mud,

stuck some way.

As I look up

I see a crack in the sky.

A glimmer of light,

I reach up high.

My emotions are spread

far and wide

on a wave,

flying high.

I keep reaching up

my hand held high,

that time has come,

to let it in,

little by little,

the beginning of a new life again.

How to use this book

You can use this book as an oracle book for guidance.

You can hold the book close to your heart and ask the angels for general guidance as you start or end your day.

If you need guidance on a situation you can ask like this:

> Dear ANGEL (name the Angel if you wish) tell the Angel about the situation …. ask for the guidance….

Then open the page where it falls and read the message in either a quote or a prayer. When you have finished reading, say: "So be it."

This book is also a fantastic resource to pray to the Angels. This connection can happen whenever you want it too.

You can choose which Angel prayer you would like to say and what Angel you would like to connect with.

You can pick a random prayer, and it may just be the message you need to hear.

Or you can take the book and say a prayer morning and evening or whenever you wish.

The prayers are beautiful, powerful, enlightening and have a message to give.

My book of Angels (Volume 2) will have more in-depth knowledge about the angels and the gifts they bring and areas they can support and help.

There will also be free downloadable meditations with the book that will help you connect with each Angel.

Hold this book close to your heart, nourish it treasure it, as it comes with love and guidance from the angels above.

Rainbow Messages from The Angels of Light

ANGELS ON THE BLUE RAY OF LIGHT

Guide and protect me day and night.

Fill me with courage and strength as I go.

Release all the worries and let the peace flow.

Let the calming blue light release all my tears and replace them with happiness and lots of good cheer.

Smiling happily as I go, feeling safe and secure as you show me the way with sparkles of blue, I know I'm ok.

Finding my ground with love as my guide as you raise me high.

I can fly,

I can fly,

I can fly.

Amen.

*I move easily
and accept the
changes that are
happening within me
and around me.*

ARCHANGEL MICHAEL

Archangel Michael on the blue ray of light

Protect and guide me day and night.

Protect my family, my home, my car, all I possess and shield me in the light of bliss.

Let your divine light surround me, always releasing my fears as you cut them away.

Your sword of light is a magical tool as you clear I stand tall after it all.

Sparkles of light shining so bright, pockets of gold for us all to hold.

Any pain that I have is taken away as I trust and believe in your strength every day.

Filled with courage and confidence, now strong and at peace, I'm so happy now.

Amen.

*See the
sunshine
in every
day*

ANGELS ON THE PINK RAY OF LIGHT

I see you come towards me, radiant and
bright.

I see your wings reach high in the sky
large and soft spreading out wide.

Floating around angelic and light.

My breath is taken as I see this sight.

Joyfully flying up and down soaring in
circles as you go round.

Angels on the pink ray of light show me the
gifts to help me take flight: love, truth and
compassion, a key to the door.

Unlock it now, and you'll suffer no more.

A message so strong for me to hear leading
me forward as the Angel's cheer.

Thankyou angels as you guide me today

I feel very special as you show me the
way.

Amen.

Today
I choose
peace

ARCHANGEL CHAMUEL

Archangel Chamuel open my heart to heal my wounds

As pain and sorrow cuts right through.

Release any grief or hurts that I hold as I know I am stuck till the love starts to flow.

As your light shines in, nurturing me strong,

I know you care as you carry me along.

A new life for me as I start freshly to decide to open to harmony,

I allow the solutions to come to me, as you help me grow on this love light I see.

I receive compassion and truth as I go and rectify anything that serves me no more.

Letting go of it all, a heavy load I know I am loved from the light above.

Amen.

*Focus on
the good
whatever you
focus on grows*

ANGELS ON THE GREEN RAY OF LIGHT

Angels on the green ray of light, nurturing
and kind loving and bright.

Flood my being, heal all my cells, fill my
heart with a watering well.

Let it spill over down into my crown as it
moves through my body all the way down.

Covering me fully from head to toe as I feel
the vibration strong as it goes.

Overflowing my organs cells and my brain
healing and restoring my health once
again.

Oh, angels on the green ray of light

I am so grateful to have you in my life.

Amen.

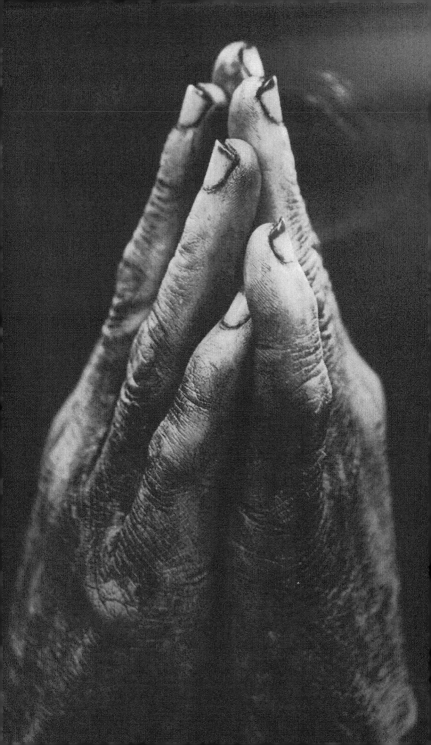

A heart
full of love
is a
golden light
only you can
find that light

ARCHANGEL RAPHAEL

Archangel Raphael with your full, green light, nurturing and calm, beautiful and bright,

I call on you daily to enlighten my mind clearing my thoughts to be nurturing and kind.

My body needs rays of healing light, and my spirit will lift to a vibration so bright.

I am in the green light. I am in the green light.
I am in the green light, with the waters of life.

I'm cleansed, and I'm clean every cell that I see is restored back to health so happy and bright.

I'm rich and I'm nurtured, peace enters me. I'm calm and healthy. I'm alive, and I'm free.

Thankyou Raphael as you mind me well.

Amen.

Find moments
of laughter
good humour
and fun
lifting our spirit
will help us
along.

NIGHT PRAYER FOR THE ANGELS

Angels of light be with me tonight

Bringing me hope as I rest from the day.

Release all my worries stresses and strains.

Let me be calm at the end of the day.

Amen.

Release our fears
anxieties and worries.
Replace them
with thoughts
of wellbeing

GUARDIAN ANGEL SHINING BRIGHT

May my dreams be magical as I rest tonight.

As I lighten my load and you clear the way for harmony and peace at the end of the day.

Amen.

Notice your
thoughts today
as they come and go.
Let them be positive
kind and nurturing
for you

ANGELS ON THE WHITE RAY OF LIGHT

Guard me, shield me, and heal me tonight.

Surround me in that vibration of light a
light so bright that fills my soul and lifts me
to a land unknown.

Where healing happens with lots of love

I waken to the morning light

Strong and healthy, vibrant and bright.

Amen.

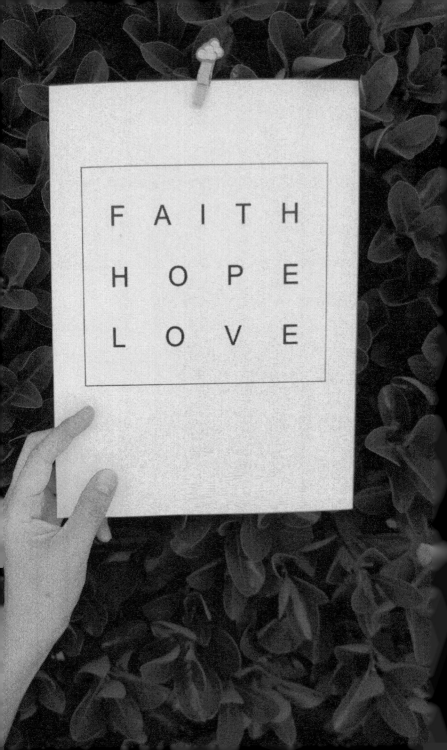

May you
be surrounded
by kind people
kind words
happy moments
and
nice memories.

PRAYER

Angels of healing, surround me with light.

Bring me peace all through the night.

Put four angels on the posts of my bed
guide and protect me as I lay my head.

Where blessings will shower me and rays of
light as I wake to a new day fresh and
bright.

Amen.

Believe in magic.
Start with you.
Magical things happen
When you believe
In you

PRAYER

Angels of light, shining so bright, show me
the way all through the night.

Guide and protect me, shower me down,
wrap me in golden as I rest now.

Amen.

*Remember
the mind will believe
everything you tell it.
Feed it well.
Positive thoughts,
kindness
and love.*

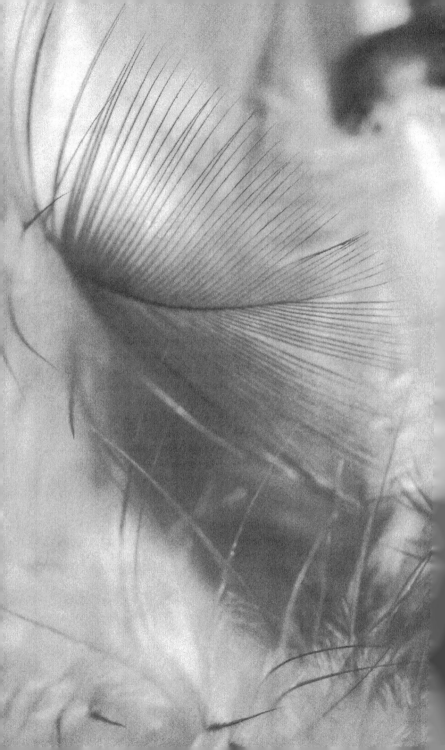

ANGEL PRAYER TO HEAL THE HEART.

Angels of the healing light, wrap your
wings round me tonight.

Lift the sorrow from my heart

Lift it away

Never to stay as its replaced by the
freshness of a new day.

Amen.

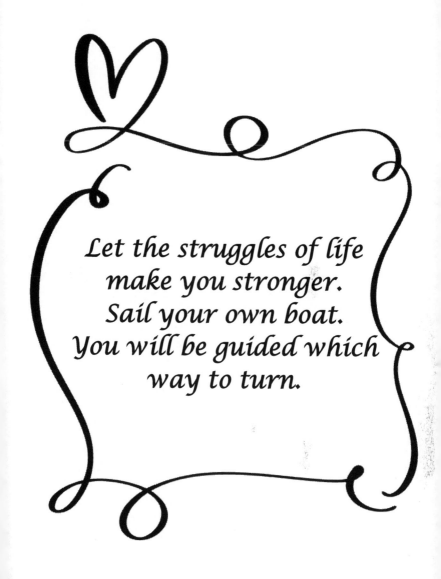

Let the struggles of life
make you stronger.
Sail your own boat.
You will be guided which
way to turn.

ANGELS ON THE YELLOW RAY OF LIGHT

Awaken me now to the energy of life.

Open my mind to all I can see

Full of ideas and creativity.

Projects and plans have a part to play, inspiration will come as you show me the way.

A light bulb is lit shining bright, where clarity and thinking will come overnight.

Thank you, oh angels on this pale-yellow light, optimistic and clear, shining so bright.

Awaken me to a new way of life with ease as I flow day and night.

Amen.

*Silence
is not empty.
It is golden
and
full of answers.*

ARCHANGEL URIEL

Archangel Uriel show me the way as your light guides me, I see many things I could not see.

Help me with clarity, a clear open mind to ideas and ways to set myself free.

Life is for living, you show me how to help me with changes in my life right now.

Hope is the answer and belief in me as you show me a new way to simply be.

Drop into my heart and expand it now as I release all that serves me no more, and happiness falls at my door.

A new beginning is part of the plan where wisdom and knowledge are shown to me; I open to my creativity.

Thank you, Uriel, on this pale-yellow light for being my guide steady and bright.

Amen.

Sun shines on everyone.

ANGELS ON THE ORANGE RAY OF LIGHT

I see sparkles, vibrant and bright.

Glowing so strong in the golden orange light, a truly precious, beautiful sight.

Surround me with your joyful cheer, laughing and playing as you draw near.

You take my hand, and I leave the ground as you lift me high, I'm so happy to fly.

I'm glowing all round from head to toe as I swirl and dance and sing as I go.

I give my worries and cares to you as you show me how to love me too.

Open my heart with fun and laughter; it's ok to be this way.

Amen.

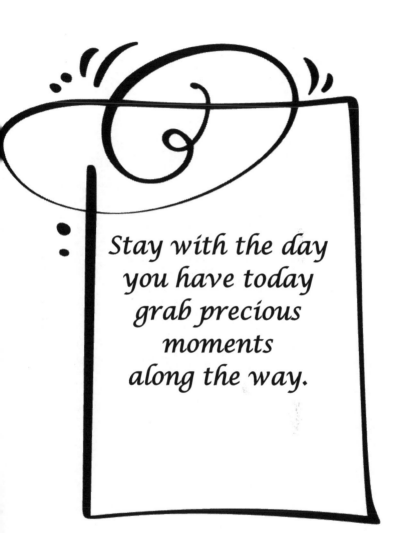

Stay with the day
you have today
grab precious
moments
along the way.

ARCHANGEL JOPHIEL

Archangel Jophiel, shining so bright with flashes of golden yellow, orange light.

An uplifting energy a feminine kind, a fragrance so sweet, as petals fall right down at her feet.

Get rid of the clutter is the message she brings, go out clear your space as she opens her wings.

Throw open the windows the doors of your home, let the breath of fresh air sweep you along.

The smell of the trees, the songs of the birds, the sun, moon and stars, the beauty of earth.

My thoughts are releasing down memory lane as flashes of joy come back once again.

Fun and laughter carefree and light, playing with daisy chains dancing all night.

I connect with the joy that all of this brings, the highest vibration as Jophiel sings.

Amen.

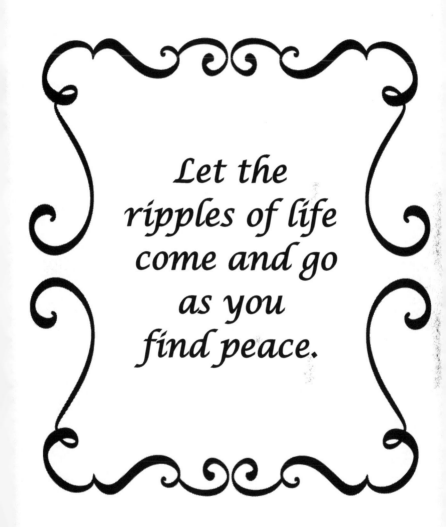

Let the
ripples of life
come and go
as you
find peace.

ANGELS ON THE RED RAY OF LIGHT

I see you in a crimson flame full of passion,
a love so real, opening my heart as I
breathe it in, I'm so blessed to be here with
you once again.

My passion is ignited as I walk through the
door, as feathers surround me and fall onto
the floor.

Your wings expand widely, covering me
down. I feel safe and secure as you
surround me now.

This light runs right through me with
passion and strength, right into my roots
as I'm connected again.

Mother Earth I am whole, and I am here.

Fully present, supported, rooted so clear,
into the earth, I stand tall. The love I feel is
deep and real.

Amen.

Moments are precious.
Moments are real.
Stay with them all
you will remember
how you feel.

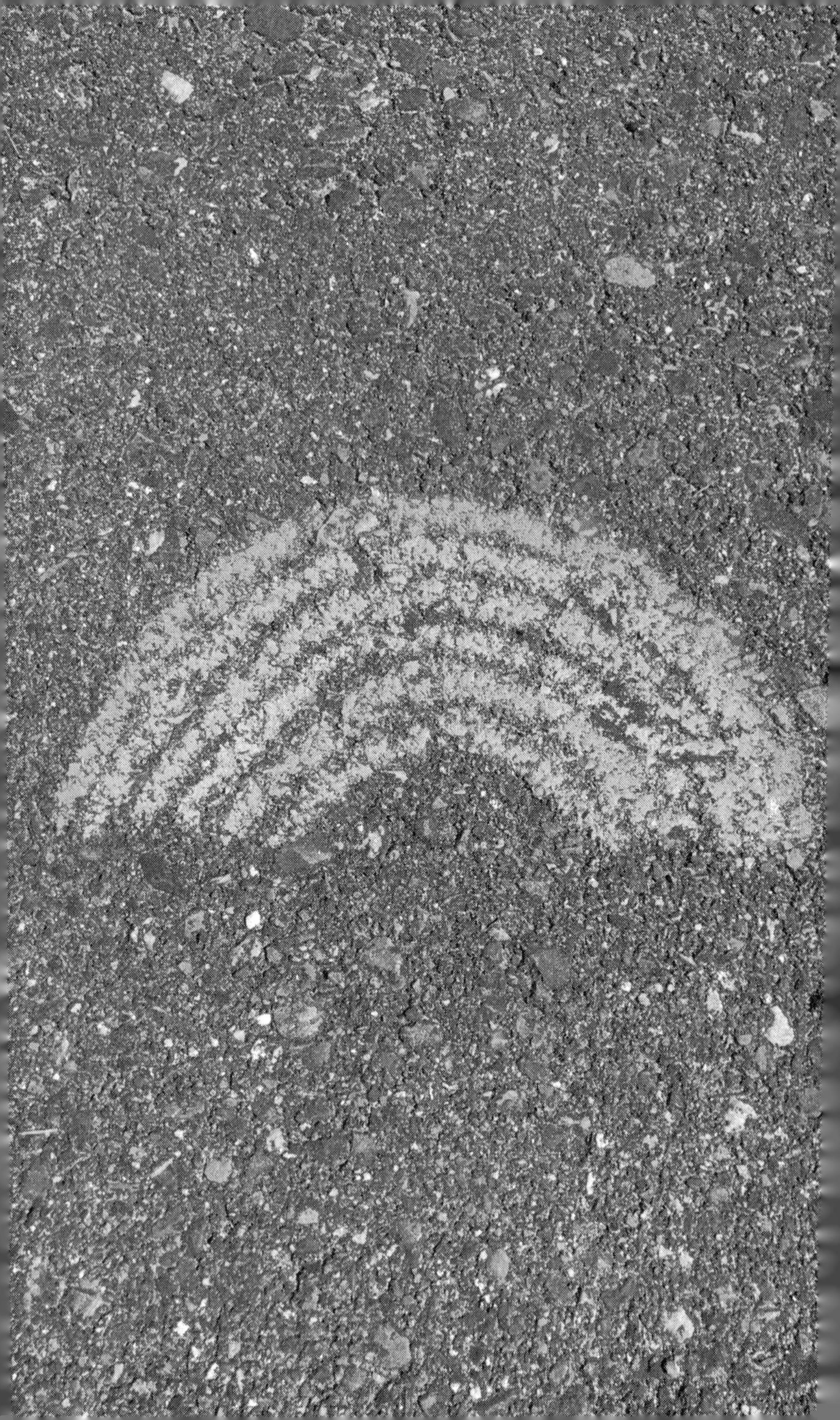

ARCHANGEL RAZIEL

Archangel Raziel, on the rainbow bridge of light, flashes of colour shining so bright.

I see a wise old wizard in a halo of gold, with rainbow colours flowing down to the toes.

The knowledge and wisdom you hold in your heart, as sparkles of light, sprinkle so strong, as you open your wings wide and long.

I feel deep healing as you draw near, a fusion of light shines into my heart; I understand now why I am here.

You help me to grow oh Angel so wise, as my body and soul lifts up, and I rise.

A vibration of love and light I can be, to help myself and humanity.

Amen.

Gentleness
is the
best
medicine
you can
give yourself.

ARCHANGEL RAZIEL OF RAINBOW LIGHT

Archangel Raziel of rainbow light, you tell
me how I need to let go, of traumas and
pain, past memories that come back again
and again.

Memories from past lives, hover round me,
teach me to let go of them completely.

Let the tears flow, release and let go,
as I feel the warmth of your comforting
glow.

As you hold me tight, I feel the divine light,
the strength within is breathtaking.

Thankyou archangel Raziel for helping me
see the power I have within me.

Now I move forward with my dreams and
my plans, as you guide me, I'm happy to
see the wisdom and knowledge within me.

Amen.

*Focus
on the good
that's within us
and
around us
today.*

ARCHANGEL HANIEL

Dear Haniel, with your halo of white, gracefully showing me the full moon in flight.

Guide me to let go of all of my fears. As I release and transmute them, I can feel clear.

I bathe in the moonlight. I feel your support. I feel lighter and lighter as the baggage drops off.

Thank you oh Haniel, for the support you give me my mind, my body, my soul, is free.

Your comforting light illuminating so bright as thoughts come in for a new way of life.

I love and thank you for the gifts you give me, to help me see mine, as the moonlight shines.

Amen.

Love
the life
you have.
Live
the life
you love.

ARCHANGEL ARIEL

Assist me right now to my purpose of life,
help me to connect to my divine light.

Lovingly show me the truth and the way to
act with integrity as I go on my way.

Help me to manifest my dreams I have
dreamed, my desires and passions for us
all to see.

As I stand in my power, I feel your lioness
strength, surrounding me with confidence.

You bring me comfort as I see your light
pink and flowing with sparkles of white.

No more questions about my plan as I step
up and take hold of the life that will be,
prosperity and abundance are waiting for
me.

Amen.

Create
beautiful
memories

ARCHANGEL RAGUEL

Dear Archangel Raguel, I see your pale blue light, vibrating so high, bringing peace and comfort as you go by.

Angel of Hope as you help me see, what is happening around me.

Balance in order as you show me the way, my thoughts and goals, ideas for me, I trust divine timing will set me free.

Amen.

*Today
I will do
something
that brings me joy
relaxes me
and makes me
feel good.*

ARCHANGEL RAGUEL

Archangel Raguel bring into my life,
energies that will help me vibrate a white
light.

Angel of relationships of all kinds, bring
like-minded souls to connect with me and
form a love that's deep and real.

Friendships and romance, a spark of the
divine, as business will flourish with the
people I meet, and love will take hold of all
things I see.

I tune into myself as I find peace.

I nurture the love that's within me.

I open to justice, respect for all, fair play
and forgiveness as I stand tall.

I trust and use honesty together we'll rise.
As I play a big part, I find a new heart.

Amen.

Kindness starts with you

ARCHANGEL RAPHAEL

Archangel Raphael as I lay down to sleep,
shine your light to heal me.

I feel your nurturing presence tonight, fill
all my cells, restore them to life.

As I open to diet and food to help me, a
detox, a cleanse, a clearing for me.

Raphael, stay with me all through the
night, help me see as I go, the actions to
take to bloom and grow.

Send me physicians of body and mind, to
help me change habits of a lifetime.

As you give me courage and strength as I
go, I renew myself to a sparkling glow.

Happy and bright blooming and radiant in
the sunlight.

Amen.

We are
all unique
and radiate
our own way.
Many shades
makes life
interesting.

ARCHANGEL MICHAEL

Archangel Michael open your wings, as I follow my path as you support me.

Let courage and strength take the lead, as my fears drop away. I'm lighter each day.

You help me to follow my purpose in life, as I know confidently this way is for me.

Your shield in your hand, your sword of light, magically helping me, day and night.

Surround me in energies that's high and bright, release any negative ones in my life.

I call on you daily for your support; I know you will be there.

I thank you for your wonderful care.

Amen.

*Spread
the love
around today
fill all
the hearts
that*

cross your way.

ARCHANGEL MICHAEL

Archangel Michael as I go on my travels of land, air and sea I call upon you to protect me.

Protect my belongings and all that I bring, so a smooth outcome happens for me.

Protect my car as I travel around, I'm safely protected from dangers round me, as I gracefully move easily.

I decide to be happy and grateful for all and enjoy myself wherever I go.

May my mind be clear, and positive thoughts fill the air.

Thank you, Archangel Michael, for your amazing light, as I call upon you, my mind is at ease, as I know you're here protecting me.

Amen.

*Life
is a sea
of change
ebbing and
flowing
as it goes.*

ARCHANGEL JOPHIEL

Archangel Jophiel as you approach me,
your beauty I see, help me to see the
beauty in me.

Beautify my thoughts so I will receive, the
life of joy that's waiting for me.

My mind is bright. It's safe for me to
attract others, so they notice me.

A spark of the divine, full of life, radiant
and bright as I see the light, I know now I
desire a beautiful life.

I take special care to care for me, my hair,
my body, the clothes I wear, a fragrance so
sweet fills the air.

The deep peace within me radiates in my
heart, as I show loving kindness,
compassion for me, a life of happiness is
waiting for me.

Amen.

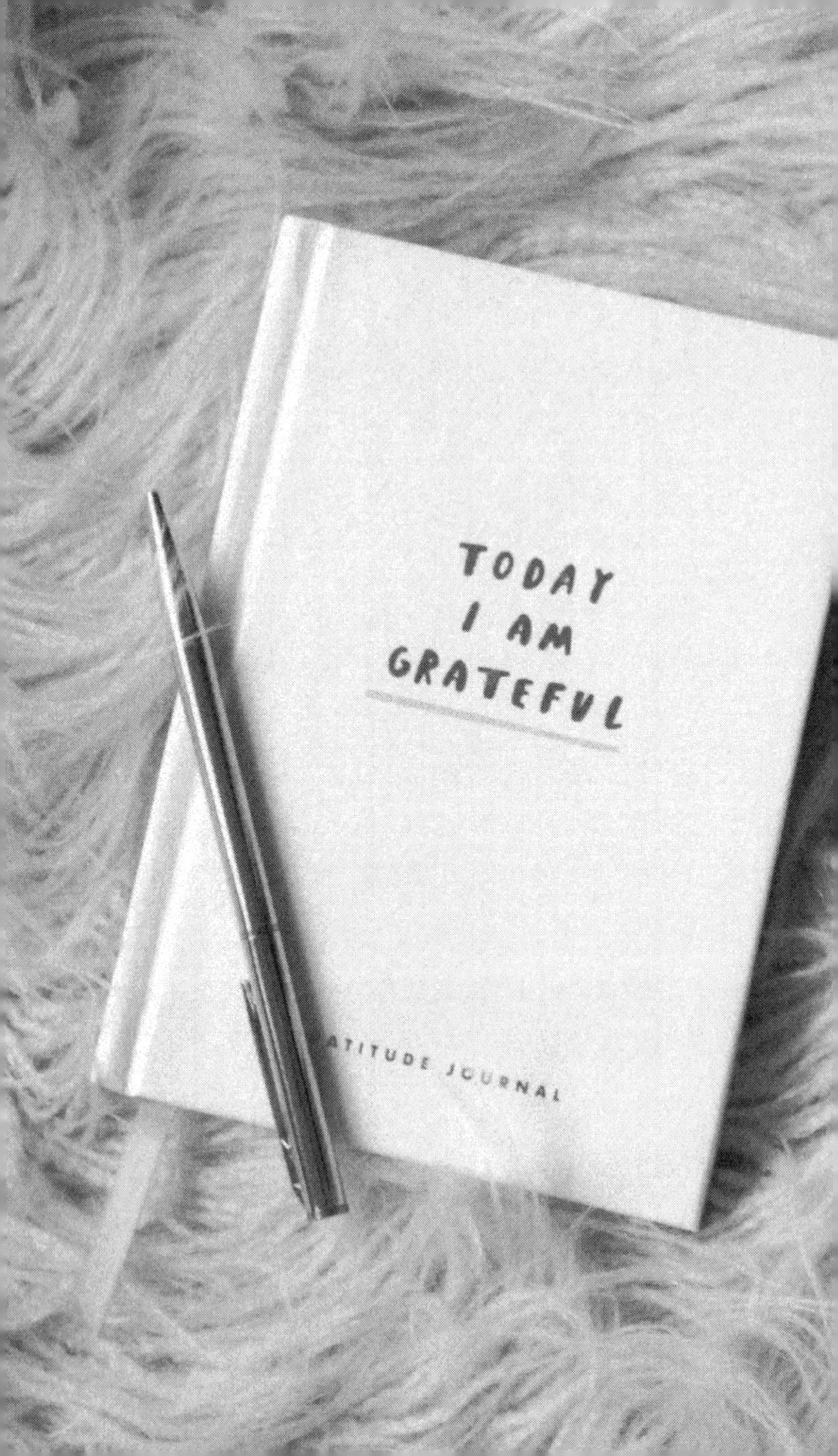
TODAY
I AM
GRATEFUL
ATITUDE JOURNAL

Grateful hearts
beat stronger
feel lighter
and
become happier.

ARCHANGEL ARIEL

Archangel Ariel, as you sit with me a harmonious feeling surrounds me.

I open to blessings of mother earth, as you show me, Ariel, this life on earth.

I stand on the ground, barefooted and tall

I'm connected.

I'm connected.

I'm connected to all.

Animals surround me, giving unconditional love, while crops, flowers and plant life bloom from above.

As you give me the insight to play my part in keeping the environment in my heart.

I'll help all I can to keep a vibrant light where all that surrounds me is happy and bright.

I am so grateful Archangel Ariel for helping me see a healthy environment is the place to be.

Amen.

I am
full of energy
boundlessly creative
and
I am
moving forward
in harmony
and peace.

ARCHANGEL SANDALPHON

Dear Archangel Sandalphon,

thank you for coming to help me see how powerful prayer in my life can be.

Day or night any time at all a simple word and my prayer is heard.

A conversation, communication to let you know my cares and worries as I go.

An idea, a thought, a feeling for me, a vision you'll show me as you support me.

You tell me the angels on the pure ray of light are waiting and open to help, day and night.

Thank you Sandalphon on the ruby-red light, an energy of fire vibrant and bright.

Amen.

Relax
Let go
Release
and
surrender.

ARCHANGEL SANDALPHON

Angel of music, a melody so sweet, I hear chimes, celestial music, peaceful and sweet.

Help me in my music career, to write songs, and play music for all to hear.

Give me platforms to present to the world as vibrations are raised, and harmony is heard.

A magical connection with all of mankind; a healing that happens from the music they find.

Thankyou Archangel Sandlaphon for the blessings you give me, creating music to help others see.

A magic bright light, a joy, a transition, a new life begins, as people tune in.

A blessing to all, music can bring, happiness and peace, a love deep within.

Amen.

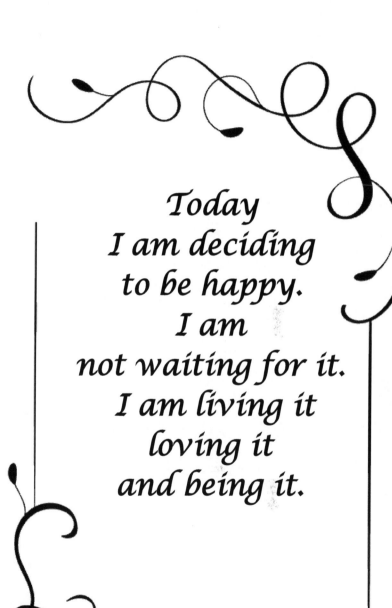

Today
I am deciding
to be happy.
I am
not waiting for it.
I am living it
loving it
and being it.

ARCHANGEL AZAREL

Dear Archangel Azarel,

thank you for helping our loved ones pass
over to the higher realms of light.

To raise them up, as they journey back, to
a place they know, and have been before.

A flashing light of purple and white, a deep
sensation, adjusting them to a new
vibration.

Reuniting their souls to all that's above, a
divine spark of peace and love.

Amen.

Angels
above
of love
and light,
be with me
as I rest tonight,
lighten my load
brighten my way,
bring peace and calm
for another day
Amen

DEAR AZAREL

You send me signs from above, to let me
know my loved ones are safe, protected
and minded in their new space.

Happy they are in a peaceful place,
watching us from the light above, and
guiding us to a life of love.

A connection I hold that's deep and strong,
a simple word, a prayer, a song.

I hold you steady in my heart, as a new
way begins, I focus my heart on the flower
within.

A flower of love, compassion and truth, as I
move to new changes, the light shines
through.

A natural process, a beginning, an end, as
the life cycle goes, Azarel you're amazing
with your healing support.

Amen.

Thank you,
God for another day,
Whatever it brought,
I've learned today.
Thank you
for the moon and stars,
Watching me sleep
at the end of the day.
Amen

DEAR AZAREL

Comfort me in my time of loss, a pain I feel cuts right through, throbbing and stabbing as my heart hurts too.

A blanket of healing falls upon me, as you clothe me in your loving arms, you comfort me, in sorrow I grieve.

You hold me in love as you show me how to honour the grief I feel now.

Release all anger, resentment and fear. As I let it go, my emotions will flow.

A wave sweeps through me, healing my heart.

I know you're safe in a special place, as the angels of light hold you tight.

I trust, and I know as I go, your spirit surrounds me, and will always be, an eternal love just for me.

Amen.

Angels be with me as I go to sleep,
May I rest in peace, and rainbows of
magic happen for me.
As I dream tonight may I receive
healing, as faith hope and love are signs
from above.
As I wake in peace, and loving light, I
know when I dream, there's a message
for me.
Amen.

ARCHANGEL RAPHAEL

Please assist me in my healing career, to
draw a mentor to guide me here.

Many teachers to teach me, and tools for
me, to open to healing and harmony.

Knowledge and learning are part of the
course, as I find a connection to the god
light source.

Bringing healing modalities in many forms,
a gift for me as I move on.

The god in me sees the god in you.

A light I can shine, to help others to be,
and how they can open their light just like
me.

Thankyou Raphael, as you help me to be, a
teacher, a guide, to help all in need.

I'm blessed and supported with the love
you give me.

Amen.

Walk easy today

PRAYER FOR LIGHTWORKERS

Dear Raphael,

Guide all lightworkers on this planet earth, all your starseeds, earth angels and spiritual beings.

We are blessed to have you on this earth to heal.

Pure connection to all, the nature, the source,

A gathering together, a full life force.

Loving each other with kind words and support, as you shine gods light, a warm-hearted presence, a gentle approach, to show the way as others take note.

Eradicating the negative, the ego, the greed, the fear, the guilt, has no place to be.

As we learn from our lessons with experience and grace, our life purpose is waiting, as we open our hearts, our minds and our souls, a new way to be, as we choose fully, to follow in the footsteps of the Angel above,

Oh, Raphael, you're so precious and truly loved.

Amen.

*I open my heart
to heal my wounds
To let love in
So, I can begin*

ARCHANGEL GABRIEL

I see an orange copper gold light, coming towards me, fiery and bright.

I hear a trumpet loud and clear, with messages for me filling the air.

Nurture your child gift from above, as they've chosen you, show them great love.

As loving parents, you'll guide them along and show them ways to be responsible and strong.

You'll teach them independence to spread their wings, free will and the choices they make will be part of the road that they will take.

They will learn lessons big and small, life is unique for them all.

With love in your hearts, a job well done, your link to their heart will never be gone."

Thank you, Gabriel, with the messages for me, in my parenting role as you guide me. The bond with my child is precious and deep as a copper-gold light hovers round me.

Amen.

As I open my eyes
to a brand-new day,
I feel the fresh air,
a new beginning,
a new spark of life,
so grateful
I have another day
in my life.

DEAR METATRON

Thank you for showing your presence to me,

a deep pink light shining so bright,

flowing the energy of the pure divine light.

You hold in your hand a Merkabah cube,

cleaning my chakras as the rays shine through.

You clear any thoughts from my crown,

as the crystal light floods right down.

You help me see what's best for me as I open to my sensitivity.

Beware of any energies around you now that are residing in you as you go round.

Use the protection of the divine light to guide and mind you day and night."

Thankyou Metatron for that message for me, as I call on that light especially for me.

Amen.

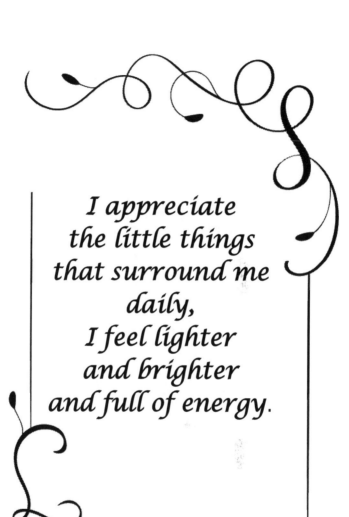

*I appreciate
the little things
that surround me
daily,
I feel lighter
and brighter
and full of energy.*

DEAR METATRON

I see your chariot in a deep pink light, with purple and green stripes.

A crimson flame of burning light, your arms outstretched standing tall looking down upon us.

You bring a message loud and clear Follow your divine purpose while you are here.

This will bring happiness of a new kind; your heart will leap, you will soar high, as you find the true beauty you have inside.

Your role will involve children, high-sensitive beings who will need your care, with schoolwork and change, to clear and detox any negative ways.

The environment you provide will be happy and bright to lessen the anxieties they carry inside.

Thankyou Metatron, for such powerful words.

As you support me, I move easily.

Amen.

I build
my foundation
of nurture and love
as this is the path
I will walk upon.

DEAR METATRON

Thank you for showing me the flower of life, as you guide me along my path of life.

You help me to see a life full of love, happiness, and peace from the divine light above.

You tell me to teach my spiritual truths, to help all others find their own Truth.

You help me find platforms to go out to the world, with knowledge and information to help heal the world.

Through study and determination, I will stand tall.
As I give my gifts to one and all.

Thank you, Archangel Metatron, for clearing the way,
Showing me fulfilment, as I move today.

Amen.

May the wind
blow through
my hair.
Love fills my heart,
and angels
surround me

everywhere.

DEAR ARCHANGEL RAPHAEL,

Open my heart to the flower within,

So I can see the beauty I hold within.

Release my emotion with a gentle wave,

Bringing comfort and peace and healing again.

Amen.

Today I choose to see
the beauty in me.
I choose to be happy
and carefree.
I let go of the worries
that are around me.

ARCHANGEL RAPHAEL

Love from above

clear my energy with your love.

As the day closes in, I need to check in,

to see what I need to energise me.

Pour your healing light

all shades of green,

flowing right down

throughout my being.

Let healing happen

as you guide me

to help me

protect my energy field.

AMEN.

A heart
full of love
will flourish
and grow.

DEAR ARCHANGEL ZADKIEL

Clothe me in your purple light,
As you shine bright, what a magical sight.

Release any fears that are holding me
down,

So I can trust, and happily see,
a joy, a love, fall over me.

You give me comfort,

I rest in sleep,

a beautiful peace surrounds me.

Amen.

*I open my heart
to the angels
for comfort
support
and healing.*

The angels tell me
to simply just be,
rest
and take moments of quiet
and peace.

This will open my connection,
to the angels above,
who are waiting to help
and send guidance to me.
I am grateful

For the moments that are given to me,
this way of life will help me feel free.

Each day, each hour,
each moment is real.

Whatever happens
and presents to me,

I will receive,
and simply just be.

Amen.

*Give yourself
a hug,
you are
amazing.*

LIVE FULLY
CREATE HAPPINESS
SPEAK KINDLY
HUG DAILY
SMILE OFTEN
HOPE MORE
LAUGH FREELY
SEEK TRUTH
INSPIRE CHANGE
LOVE DEEPLY

DEAR ARCHANGEL CHAMUEL

Comfort me in times of stress,
Release my anxieties as I rest.

Help me to see what's right for me,
as I make changes to help me.

Wrap me in your blanket of pink
to heal my emotions as I sleep.

Show me ways to create new things,
regaining my power,
helps me see what I must do
for my souls' needs.

Thank you Chamuel,
as I find my heart,
the love within me
will guide me,
to the place that I should be.

Amen.

Love is patient,
Love is kind,
Love is real,
Love is eternal,
Love is everywhere,
Look inside,
you will be surprised
what you will find.

DEAR ARCHANGEL GABRIEL

Messenger of the light nurturing and kind,
as you come to me in a golden sunshine.

My childhood memories flood back to me
as pain and sorrow I feel deep.

Take hold of that child you once were, give
it all the love you deserve.

Bring it on play trips, nice things to do
skipping and dancing as you laugh too.

Hold the child's hand as you walk through
the meadow, feel the gold sunshine around
as you move.

Healing is happening as you bring in peace,
compassion and nurture as you rest easy.

Make special dates to go out and have fun,
sending love, holding hands, giving big
hugs.

You are now at peace with your inner child,
a child of love from the light above.

Amen.

When
I accept,
all the things
in my life,
it helps me
be patient, loving
and kind.

DEAR ZADKIEL

Help me to concentrate easily on the exams and studies that are facing me.

Help me to retain the focus I need to remember the facts and figures I see.

Release any stress I hold within me, to complete my studies successfully.

Show me the light I hold within, so I can see the future I hold is bright for me.

Amen.

Smiling
is contagious
let it ripple
and flow.

DEAR ZADKIEL

Open my ears to all I can hear, as you
bring messages loud and clear.

Clairaudience is part of the gifts you bring,
as I hear in a song, a prayer, a story, a
message that will enlighten me.

You ask me to take responsibility, new
choices, new ways to fill my day.

I'm healing

I'm healing

I'm healing right now as you support me
and show me how.

I forgive and let go all that I've known,
for a new wave of light to enter my life.

I love you Zadkiel for showing me,
the truth of my life
so I can see,
to act from a place of integrity.

Amen.

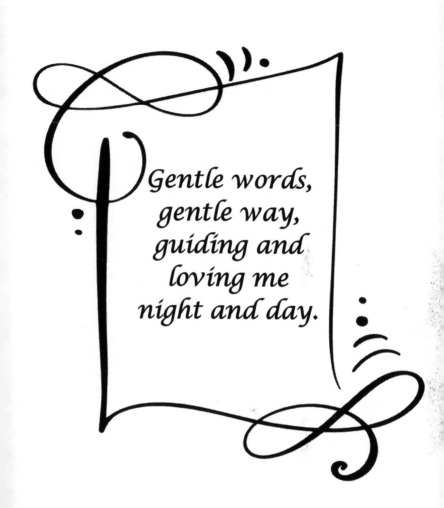

Gentle words,
gentle way,
guiding and
loving me
night and day.

DEAR JEREMIEL

Angel of hope, Angel of dreams, help me to remember all that I see.

You give me clairvoyance to inspire me, to see my guides that surround me.

You vibrate on a deep purple light with flashes of orange radiant and bright.

You ask me to do a life review as you swirl around me, the brighter I see.

You show me memories of past events, I see now in my life, it's time for me to open to ways to change and heal.

You guide me on a healing light, to see my lessons in full flight.

I gather them all with love as I go, I see them as blessings as my heart unfolds.

Amen.

May I have peace,
May I have compassion,
May I have support,
May I have loving
kindness,
As I go on my way.

DEAR JEREMIEL

Thank you for being my amazing guide as
your presence is subtle, caring, and kind.

A lotus flower you hold in your hand,
blooming with a purple, orange glow,

Radiant and bright so sweet and light.

You show me how, with great difficulty,
this flower emerged from the depths of the
sea.

A muddy patch, dark and deep, pushed its
way up towards the light you see.

I bring the gift of peace and love as you
know I am here, to guide you along.

The strength and courage to rebirth and
regrow is within us all as we go.

I bring the gift of peace and love as you
know, I am here to guide you along.

Amen.

Stand back
and just be,
that will free me
to a place
of serenity.

GUARDIAN ANGEL

Oh, guardian angel,
my strength and my guide

Help me to see my abilities
to change my career
to one that serves me.

To provide for me financially,
to have a good life
with my family.

To give me abundance
in health
and wellbeing.

To do my work honestly.

Amen.

Finally

I offer personal Angel Card Readings with Angelic guidance.

I also offer mindfulness and meditation to learn and perfect the art, and how one can connect with that inner space and peace within for healing.

Working with the healing energy of Reiki, Rahanni and Bio energy at all levels and I offer one to one healings, either physically in person or on an online platform.

I hold qualifications in all of the above.

I am so happy to offer help and the art of healing, and how the therapies above can help to open our hearts to heal and grow and develop and bring new change.

I can devise a programme for each individual client, depending on their needs.

I am in the process of creating an online course all about the angels and Angel therapy.

To avail of any of my services you can connect with me personally through my website at

www.melissashealing.ie

or on Facebook at Melissa's healing.

Life is always evolving,
so are we.
Change is inevitable,
exciting and real.

Love and Blessings to you all.

Melissa